CAMPAIGN STAFF

As exhausting as campaigning for president is, campaigning for a campaign can be even more tiring. We cannot list all the people who have helped us with this effort, but without the following folks, your campaign effort could never have gotten off the press.

Thanks to Gary, Caryl, Miguel, Rose, Kelly, Lollie, Stuart Alan, Carmen, Fran and John.

Our very special thanks to Betty and Gary Ball, Rob Pudim, Michael Cader, Peter Livingston and all our friends at Workman Publishing.

See you on the campaign trail!

CONTENTS

READY, SET, GO

FROM RAGS TO RICHES

THE HOME STRETCH

About the Presidential Seal

Executive Order 11649 requires permission from the current president to use the Presidential Seal. To make a long story short, Reagan's office said no. Rather than fight the bureaucracy, we decided that the Everybody for President Campaign needed its own seal—of the people, by the people, for the people. We ask only that you promise in advance to let everybody use your seal after you're elected.

READY, SET, GO

THE PRESIDENTIAL SEAL
EVERYBODY FOR PRESIDENT
"THE BUCK
STOPS HERE"

Everybody Who?

With all the money and attention lavished on the presidential campaign every four years, it's astonishing how few Americans decide to run. All the fanfare is focused on those fellows (there's not a female among them) who make the most noise about their candidacy, as most of us sit back and watch. Few Americans even vote for President, let alone run.

It's time for a change. Democracy can be more than just a spectator sport. The much maligned American Dream is far more accessible than is generally thought. Anybody—and by extension everybody—regardless of race, color, creed or qualifications can

legitimately seek the highest office in the land.

But the good-old-boys, hacks, yes men and people of privilege who form the political elite do not cotton to throwing open the gates. They choose to reserve the political arena for their own personal playground, keeping the ways and wiles of the campaign trail a deep, dark secret and making the electoral process as cumbersome as possible. Primaries, committees, conventions, press coverage, fund raising—there seem to be so many things a candidate must master in addition to acting presidential that most Americans never even consider running.

And what a shame it is. Those with the truly creative and dynamic ideas for getting America moving generally limit their speeches to cocktail parties and remain armchair politicians. Now, for the first time, average Americans can learn the secret techniques of running for president. We at Everybody for President Campaign Headquarters have unabashedly stolen every briefing book, relentlessly infiltrated every major campaign organization, tirelessly interrogated hundreds of campaign veterans and moronically watched hours and hours of television. The result is this handy, fact-filled kit containing everything you really need to run.

We felt it was our patriotic duty to make this compendium of innovative and entertaining campaign practices available to you—

we can't allow the electoral process to become just another bad television series. With high unemployment, outdated industries, wayward foreign policies and a skyrocketing deficit, it is clear that this is indeed the time for Everybody to come to the aid of their country.

Why Not Me?

By now you are probably asking yourself, "But am I qualified to run for president?"

Yes, you are—and so is your son, your dog and even your roommate from Rumania. In one of the more egalitarian quirks of the American system, there are absolutely no requirements to run for president. None. Zip.

You don't even have to be a registered voter. Eisenhower's first vote ever went to himself for president. Ironically, convicted felons aren't allowed to vote, but they can run for president. Back in 1920 Eugene Debs ran for president from prison and got close to a million votes (which is, incidentally, more votes than he ever got as a free man).

THIS ORDER PROVIDES for the forwarding of First-Class Mail and all parcels of obvious value for a period not to exceed 1 year.

Print or Type *(Last Name, First Name, Middle Initial)*

CHANGE OF ADDRESS IS FOR:
☒ Entire Family *(When last name of family members differ, separate orders for each last name must be filed)*
☐ Individual Signer Only

I AGREE TO PAY FORWARDING POSTAGE FOR NEWSPAPERS AND MAGAZINES FOR 90 DAYS
☐ NO ☒ YES

USPS USE ONLY
CLERK/CARRIER ENDORSEMENT
CARRIER ROUTE NUMBER
DATE ENTERED

OLD ADDRESS
No. and St., Apt., Suite, P.O. Box or R.D. No. (In care of)
Post Office, State and ZIP Code

NEW ADDRESS
No. and St., Apt., Suite, P.O. Box or R.D. No. (In care of)
1600 Pennsylvania Ave.
Post Office, State and ZIP Code
Washington, D.C. 20500

Effective Date
Jan 17, 1985
If Temporary, Expiration Date
Sign Here
Date Signed
Signature & title of person authorizing address change. (DO NOT print or type)

PS Form 3575, Feb. 1979

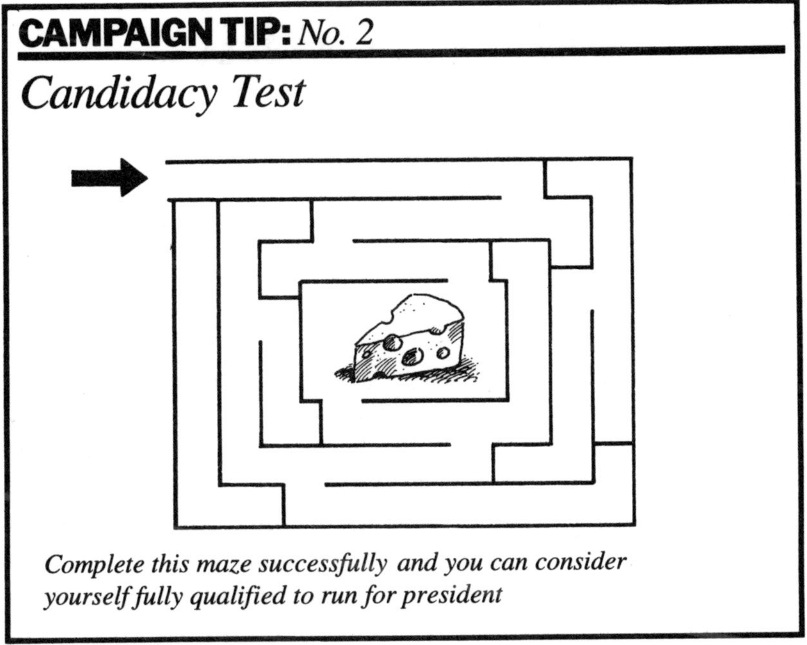

CAMPAIGN TIP: *No. 2*

Candidacy Test

Complete this maze successfully and you can consider yourself fully qualified to run for president

And Richard Nixon . . . well, never mind.

Intelligence is certainly no issue. Andrew Jackson believed the earth was flat, and Ronald Reagan keeps trying to make it that way. So, in this land of the free and the brave, truly everybody can run for president.

This does not mean you'll be allowed to take office, though. To actually *be* president the Constitution does require that you be a natural-born citizen, at least thirty-five years of age, and that you have spent no fewer than fourteen years in the United States.

Still sounds pretty skimpy, doesn't it? Experience has shown the practical advantages of being rich, white and male, but there is nothing about this in the formal rules. You don't have to be corrupt, stupid or lazy, either, but it might help. Statesmanship is optional.

The real question, then, is not whether you're qualified to run, but whether you really want to. Do you feel a calling? Are you driven by a patriotic sense of duty and service? Do you have some spare time to kill?

The Ultimate Job Hunt

Admittedly, running for president sounds like strenuous work, more a chore than an adventure. If you feel that way, try thinking of it as simply applying for a job. After all, the presidency is one of the best positions available in America (aside from being independently wealthy). The perks are great and no privilege will ever be denied you again. It's a lot like being king—you won't need to carry cash.

In light of this, running for president is a particularly appropriate pursuit for the nation's millions of unemployed. Americans have been told repeatedly by the present administration to learn new skills for the future—so what better job to train for? Pursuing the presidency is far easier than looking for a real job. No more resumés to send, interviews to attend, agencies to pay, classifieds to scan or rude brush-offs to avenge.

Instead of pounding the pavement in anonymity, you will enjoy free and frequent television coverage. Audiences, personnel directors among them, will listen to you no matter how irrelevant or irresponsible your thoughts might be. People will insist on giving you money. Furthermore, as an unemployed candidate, you can almost certainly count on the initial support of more than four million similarly unoccupied Americans.

But there is no reason to feel excluded if you already have a job. Bored housewives and burned-out executives are also ideally suited for candidacy. Running for president is

PRESIDENT
UNITED STATES
Large postindustrial nation seeks chief executive. Salary is $200,000 a year, plus $100,000 travel allowance and $20,000 entertainment. Benefits include house with staff and gorgeous view, limousine, jet, bodyguards, meals, free tickets and sporadic respect. Hours are flexible.
Dynamic pension plan includes $69,630 per year plus $96,000 office allowance, free office space and mailing privileges. Previous holders of this position have enjoyed countless business opportunities, golf tournament invitations, book contracts and libraries named in their honor. You are entitled to burial in a federal cemetery (preferably after leaving office) and a place in history. Apply now.

CAMPAIGN TIP: *No. 3*

Carry a Budget Bodyguard

This reasonably priced alternative to Secret Service protection includes a garlic clove, a whistle, a sling shot, and spare grapes. The briefcase doubles as a quick-opening, fruit resistant body shield.

eminently more fulfilling than working at the Junior League Thrift Shop. Though employers have widely varying policies concerning running for office on company time, some might even promote ambitious employees—just in case you win.

As President Reagan has so ably demonstrated, running for president is also the perfect postretirement activity. At the other end of the spectrum, young children should be encouraged to run too. "Presidential Contender, 1984" will look great one day on a college application. It should also be noted that campaigning for president will give purpose to house pets and get welfare recipients off one dole and onto another.

Watch out, baseball. America may have a brand-new national pastime.

How Right Is Your Stuff?

Running for president should be a careful, rational decision, not just a fanciful whim. Thoroughly consider the rigors before committing yourself. Are you prepared to limit yourself to just two or three months of vacation per year? Will you be able to make decisions affecting the lives of millions at the drop of a hat? Are you able to sleep soundly through crises? How skillful are you at horseback riding, golf and sailing?

Should you feel physically capable of enduring such stress for a full four-year term, we urge you to run.

The president shouldn't make the average American feel inferior. Our favorite presidents have been those with only a vague grip on reality and the self-control to not let that bother them. If you insist on carrying your intellectual baggage with you, try to keep it well concealed. There's no point in making folks nervous. Remember: the chief executive is not really an executive at all, but a father figure for the entire nation. A mother figure or even a cuddly grandmotherly sort might be better still.

You needn't worry about experience. After all, it's the experts in Washington who have gotten us where we are today. Past elections have clearly demonstrated that the electorate prefers outsiders who wave their ignorance like a banner. The time is ripe for an out-of-touch, do-nothing political nobody—or everybody—capable of letting the affairs of state collapse back into their natural condition.

I Do Declare

Once you've finished the soul-searching and have decided to run for president, the first order of business is to . . . do nothing.

That's right: nothing. The known non-candidate is often far more successful at getting support than the unknown declared candidate. By way of example, in 1980 far more people supported Ted Kennedy for president when he wasn't a candidate than when he was, and they rallied to his side again after he lost the nomination. Following that logic, you would be best off waiting until after the election to announce your candidacy, though it's not as much fun that way.

Do try to remain silent for at least the first week or two (we know this won't be easy) and wait for a mandate to build. After that, hold a minimum of three press conferences a day to adamantly deny the rumors that you are going to run. The media will be far gentler with you before your candidacy becomes official, so enjoy the honeymoon while it lasts. As the anticipation builds, the crowds should clamor: "Run, Everbody, Run."

If they don't, you haven't followed the instructions closely enough. Go back to square one and start over.

When you finally announce your candidacy, try to do it on a slow news day—Sundays are usually your best bet. Speak in the most general of terms. "Groundswell" and "responsibility" are good words to throw in. Gradually work your way toward misty visions of a bright future and the failures of the current administration. Modestly acknowledge your willingness to sacrifice personal goals and ambitions to serve your country, and don't forget to run through your exceptional qualifications; start as far back as the Scouts and drone on from there. Then pause reflectively, bow your head for a moment and see if you can get your voice to crack as you solemnly say:

"I, (your name here) , do therefore accept the challenge of the people and am now prepared to make myself available for the good of all to serve this great country as president of the United States." (This sentence of declaration has been standardized so as to avoid any unnecessary confusion, especially on the part of the press. Remember to fill in your name ahead of time.)

Don't you wish it were that easy to apply for a real job?

Red Tape

Red tape is what supporters shower on you when you win, and what the government showers on you when you run. While the trappings of bureaucracy are unavoidable, you shouldn't let mere paperwork interfere with your presidential aspirations.

You can make your campaign as big or as small as you want. Feel free to hustle contributions and spend money to your heart's content. Or, if you prefer, a low-budget to no-budget campaign can be just as much fun.

The Federal Election Commission will want to hear from you by the time you have collected a mere $5,000 in campaign contributions or have spent $5,000 on campaign expenses. Don't worry about the money you spend just "testing the waters" (which legitimately includes expenses like your "Everybody for President" campaign kit); the F.E.C. is only interested in actual campaign expenses.

If you crave official status, go ahead and file your Statement of Candidacy F.E.C. Form 2 (included in your campaign kit), even if you have no intention of collecting or spending campaign money—the government is always happy to hear from interested parties. It's a simple form, with complicated government instructions on the back. All you really have to do is fill in your name and address at the top, and write in "President" on line 4. Party affiliation is optional. Unless you are a veteran presidential candidate, leave the identification number space blank—the F.E.C. will assign you your very own candidate identification number to use in this and all future presidential campaigns.

The section called Principal Campaign Committee is for candidates who actually plan on collecting contributions and spending campaign money. You don't even need one of these committees

STATEMENT OF CANDIDACY

(see reverse side for instructions)

1. (a) Name of Candidate (in Full)

   (b) Address (Number and Street)

   (c) City, State and ZIP Code

2. Identification No.

3. Party Affiliation

4. Office Sought

5. District & State of Candidate

DESIGNATION OF PRINCIPAL CAMPAIGN COMMITTEE

6. I hereby designate the following named political committee as my Principal Campaign Committee for the ______ (Year of Election) election(s).

   NOTE: This designation must be filed with the appropriate office listed below.

   (a) Name of Committee (in Full)

   (b) Address (Number and Street)

   (c) City, State and ZIP Code

DESIGNATION OF OTHER AUTHORIZED COMMITTEES

7. I hereby authorize the following named committee, which is NOT my principal campaign committee, to receive and expend funds on behalf of my candidacy.

   NOTE: This designation should be filed with the principal campaign committee.

   (a) Name of Committee (in Full)

   (b) Address (Number and Street)

   (c) City, State and ZIP Code

I certify that I have examined this Statement and to the best of my knowledge and belief it is true, correct and complete.

(Signature of Candidate) (Date)

NOTE: Submission of false, erroneous, or incomplete information may subject the person signing this Statement to the penalties of 2 U.S.C. §437g.

CANDIDATES FOR –

President mail to:
Federal Election Commission
1325 K Street, N.W.
Washington, D.C. 20463

U.S. Senate mail to:
Secretary of the Senate
119 D Street, N.E.
Washington, D.C. 20510

U.S. House of Representatives mail to:
Clerk of the House
1036 Longworth Office Bldg.
Washington, D.C. 20515

For further information contact:
Federal Election Commission
Toll Free 800-424-9530
Local 202-523-4068

FEC FORM 2 (3/80)

F.E.C. Form 2:

Separates the candidates from the voters. The back and front have been reproduced relative to their importance.

CAMPAIGN TIP: *No. 6*

Look Right

Guaranteed not to offend anyone in key states like Iowa and New Hampshire

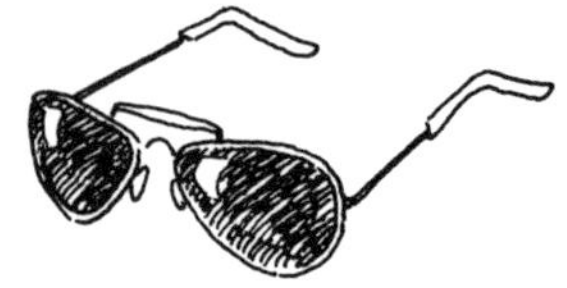

Guaranteed not to offend anyone in California

Guaranteed to intimidate

These tend to blur the issues

unless you go over the $5,000 level, but it's a nice way to involve friends who enjoy being close to power yet don't want all the responsibilities of running.

The title of your campaign committee is up to you, but it must in some way include your own name. "Tommie Jones for President Committee" is rather ordinary, so how about something like "Mary Smith's Presidential Campaign Committee and Jazz Band"? Remember to sign and date the form, and be sure to double-check your zip code—the F.E.C. frowns on the filing of false, erroneous or incomplete information.

Having your own campaign committee means you will also have to file the Statement of Organization F.E.C. Form 1 (also included in your campaign kit). Having to file Form 2 before you file Form 1 is apparently just another one of those little quirks designed to test your skills as a candidate. This form is due ten days after you officially become a candidate, even though it takes six weeks for the government to tell you this and send you the appropriate forms (aren't you glad you have a campaign kit?).

If you have any questions, just call the F.E.C. at their toll-free number (which is of course not really free, since taxpayers support those few who want to chat with the F.E.C. long distance). By the way, you are legally allowed to reproduce the form—but only the form. No sneaking in dollar bills at the same time.

Now for the real nitty-gritty. You will need a treasurer and a bookkeeper. You can fill both jobs yourself or call in a couple of trusted friends, but be forewarned: you are not allowed to either receive or spend campaign money while the office of treasurer is vacant (i.e., not filled; the intelligence of your treasurer has no legal bearing on whether or not you are allowed to spend money).

Don't be put off by this, though. According to informed sources within the F.E.C., if you plan on running a no-budget campaign (no contributions and no expenditures), you can just put a note on line 9 to that effect. If you should change your mind later, remember to file an amended form just to keep everything straight.

Oh, yes. If you decide to stop being a candidate someday, let the F.E.C. know that, too, so they can tell the computer to stop sending you campaign junk mail.

White House Workout

The campaign trail can be physically demanding. Muscles you never knew you had are liable to act up if proper precautions are not taken.

Keep in mind that running for president has absolutely nothing to do with running. The only thing you should bother to exercise regularly is your prerogative. So ignore calisthenics and don't mess with isometrics. The candidate's daily fitness regimen need only include seven of the following exercises. The nice thing is, none of them will tax you.

Once you have mastered these basic exercises, practice doing several at a time. Candidates are always on the move and must be able to do two—or preferably three—things at once.

The Suitcase Serve

You may well have to carry your own bags during the first few weeks of campaigning. Once you've accumulated a volunteer staff of sufficient size and enthusiasm, however, you needn't bother with this type of strenuous chore. All you do is reach for your bags and pause to look humble—this will make the front page of the local newspaper—and then toss them to the closest volunteer once the camera shutter has clicked. Practice will improve your aim and agility.

The Foot-in-Mouth Flip-flop

Candidates' feet have a disconcerting way of ending up in their mouths. This simple but effective yoga exercise will enable you to quickly remove the foot, do a half-twist and a hop, and start again with both feet planted firmly on the ground. With practice, you should be able to perform this move effortlessly and without being noticed, even on national television.

The Parallel Pucker

A basic presidential skill also required of candidates is the ability to speak out of both sides of the mouth.

Exercising Your Ego

Unfortunately, egos bruise easily, so handle this exercise with care. Speaking at Toastmaster breakfast gatherings and going home to Mother are among the quickest ways to build an ego. On the other hand, should you require an ego reduction program, we suggest you take two aspirin and volunteer for a brief question-and-answer period with Sam Donaldson and Ted Koppel.

Jumping to Conclusions

Because of its incriminating nature, this leap is best performed in private. Only the most experienced candidates should attempt such a delicate maneuver on the spot during debates and press conferences.

The Crisis Nap

This time-honored approach to stress will serve you well on the campaign trail and through any number of terms in the Oval Office. When all else fails, let your eyelids droop, open your mouth slightly and drift off into a stupor. When you wake up, discreetly ask where things stand and nod knowingly.

Exercising Restraint

On the other hand, restraint need only be exercised in public. Since cardiopulmonary muscles are often flexed during the attempt to find restraint, this procedure does have some stressful side effects. A stiff drink following this portion of the workout is highly recommended.

Additional Exercises

FROM RAGS TO RICHES

The Candidate's New Clothes

About the only thing in this world that changes faster than political fortunes is current fashions. Happily for the candidate, politician wear isn't subject to the dramatic swings that plague the world of mainstream fashion.

Viewers—uh, voters—expect a particular image from their candidate. They insist on a certain warmth and trustworthiness, a look that is confident but not brash, gentle but firm, youthful but

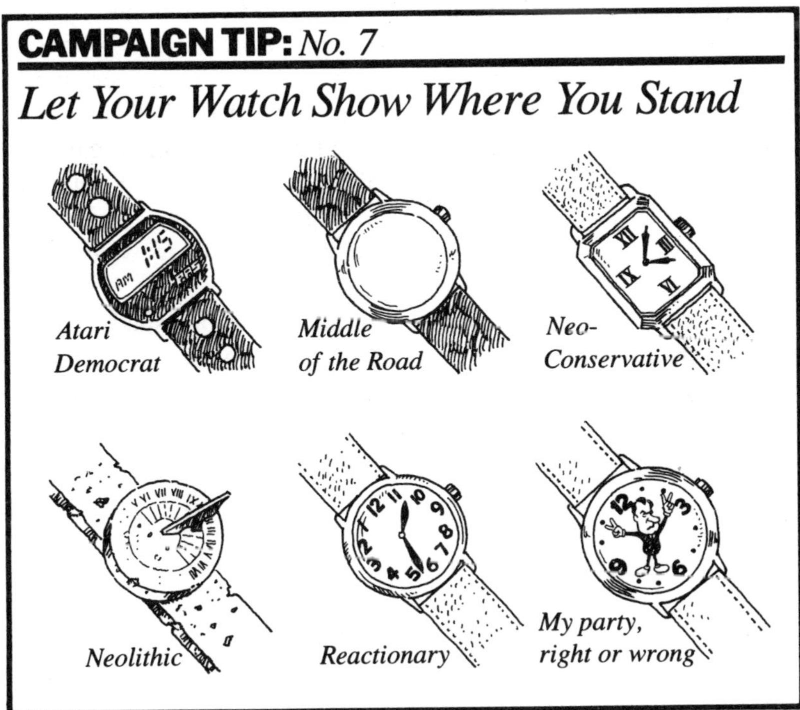

wise. Unfortunately, very few tailors make that kind of outfit. Everybody expects the president to look something like Kennedy—any Kennedy, but a Kennedy.

One way to help construct a look that will work for you is to study the dressing styles of past candidates. John Anderson always gave the appearance of someone running for president, not of someone who could actually be one. Carter was pretty well dressed the first time around, but failed to win a second term because he couldn't settle on a consistent style. Fellow Americans cringed at seeing their president in old jeans and a cardigan sweater one day and a blue suit the next. In alternating between the Plains look and Capital couture, he affected a suspicious air of unreliability.

So the first lesson in shopping for campaign clothing is, whatever you decide to wear, buy ten of the same thing. Special outfits to appeal to different parts of the electorate are one thing, but you should decide on some kind of basic uniform. To hold down costs, you might want to follow the lead of the Olympic Committee and name a clothing manufacturer's entire fall line the "Official Garments of the 1984 Everybody for President Campaign."

Since you'll spend most of your time appearing on television and will be portrayed in embarrassingly cropped newspaper photos, it's best to concentrate on the little details, the things by which people will remember you—cuff links, tie clips, hats and earrings. But don't overdo it. Rhinestone chokers, fedora hats and polka-dot bow ties will not appeal to diverse segments of the population. Americans may not have a lot of taste, but we do know what people are supposed to look like on television.

The color blue can also cause problems. Certain shades of blue will disappear on the screen due to the quirks of television special effects. This can make your head appear to be floating in space—a unique, but possibly disconcerting, image for the voters to accept.

Candidate Models

This is what everyone thinks the president should look like

This is what most people who are really qualified to be president look like

This is what the president has never looked like

Cashing In

The easiest way to raise campaign money is by selling ambassadorships and cabinet posts.

Unfortunately for the financially ambitious candidate, this ploy and nearly all the other best money-raising schemes are now illegal.

Gone are the days when presidential candidates could find their pockets stuffed with hundred-dollar bills after meeting with the good-old-boys. Nixon spoiled all the fun by going a little overboard with his slush funds and strong-arm approach to special-interest groups. It is considered wise to more or less account for your financial expenditures. Now it's illegal for any presidential candidate to accept over $100 in cash. Checks are okay up to $1,000.

The best place to troll for money these days is in the land of Political Action Committees (the latest corporate scheme for buying candidates). You don't even have to promise anything in

Even if you're desperate for funds, don't shake hands and solicit contributions at the same time

Fun With Funds

Truly the greatest joy of presidential campaigning is Federal Matching Funds. It's the government's way of encouraging you to run for president.

Here's how the game is played. First you collect $100,000 in small bills from at least twenty states. Then you fill out a few more F.E.C. forms and watch those federal tax dollars double your money.

What a deal! Instead of paying most of your hard-earned money to the government in taxes, Uncle Sam is giving you a big bonus. It's democracy in action, inflation in reverse . . . welfare for the rich and powerful. You are expected to spend that money on your campaign, of course, but every presidential candidate should have a campaign office in Vail, right?

And remember, if you get enough of the vote this year, they'll put some more money aside for you in case you want to try again. Experience does pay off.

particular—stick with vague hints and strategic winks, and the money should follow.

Another popular fund raiser is the $100- to $1,000-a-plate dinner. You might consider offering discounts to guests who bring their own dishes and making up the difference by charging extra for silverware. Mondale used a homey touch with his series of "house parties"; the first round raised a cool $4.5 million from the captive partygoers, and he didn't even have to use his own house. You might try Tupperware.

Fat Cats and Chubby Kittens

As any schoolboy knows, presidential nominations and elections used to be settled in back rooms (the back room of what, no one really knows) by a political breed called Fat Cats. Today, however, their influence has been seriously curtailed by campaign contribution limitations, and the scarcity of back rooms in our prisons.

In the old days, a Fat Cat was immediately recognizable by a distinct odor of cigar smoke and an unmistakable paunch. These days you're more likely to notice a hint of designer cologne and an all-season tan.

Instead of having to cuddle up to a few select Fat Cats, the modern presidential candidate must now keep thousands of Chubby Kittens purring and writing checks.

This is not all bad. The Fat Cats had an annoying habit of telling the candidate what to say, what to do, and who to hire for all those patronage jobs—from the cabinet on down. It's a little more difficult for a single Chubby Kitten to buttonhole the candidate for a persuasive discussion on how to run the country. There is no real harm in listening to their suggestions and maintaining a warm smile and an open mind . . . at least until the checks clear.

Full Court Press

With Phil Donahue running the candidate debates and anchormen projecting election winners before the first vote is cast, you know the balance of power in the presidential campaign has tipped in favor of Network Headquarters, not Campaign Headquarters. The polite word for reporters is "media," but as you'll soon see, "press" is a far more appropriate term. If you think the candidate is the one who runs political campaigns, think again. The only reason candidates run is that the press is chasing them.

It's not completely stacked against you, though. The candidate is definitely a celebrity (and a potential guest on *Dynasty*), and you will have to act accordingly. You are constantly competing with the various wars around the world, not to mention natural and human disasters of all varieties.

Games Reporters Play

Reporters much prefer inventing their own stories to transcribing the tedious details of the day. They realize that to make a yearlong campaign exciting they have to do a lot of the work for you.

One of their most annoying habits is to repeat inaccurate or irrelevant information until the negative associations rub off on you. Asking you to deny that you're imitating Kennedy or wondering over and over again if your connections to labor will turn off voters plants a subliminal notion in the viewers' minds that, in their more alert nonviewing hours, translates into political action. This is the classic case of media over matter.

Similarly, reporters will try to throw you off-track with absurd questions. You might be asked, "What would you do if a Czechoslovakian airliner crossed U.S. air space and headed directly for our defense command?" Don't even try to make a rational response. Look that camera in the eye, smile and say, "That's a really dumb question. Would you care to try again?"

You can always turn the tables by answering the question with a question, or finding another way to change the subject entirely, but your strongest weapon is silence. Reporters hate silence. Directors hate silence. Editors hate reporters who elicit silence. And reporters hate to be hated by their bosses.

Be particularly careful of front-runner status—this means you're next on the hit list. You'll notice that the number of front runners in any campaign is directly proportional to the total hours of television coverage. The best strategy for your peace of mind and chances for success is to avoid becoming a front runner until the last possible moment. Waiting until after the election may mean not winning, but you can have a lot more fun.

Commercials

Free coverage is best, of course, but there is still plenty of need for some paid commercials presenting you in the best possible light.

This year, candidates have shown a clear preference for the slick Madison Avenue style. Only a few have kept the boring approach of sitting in a cardboard living room and talking to the viewing voters about platforms and issues.

As an astute candidate, you know that attempting anything of true depth or serious understanding will be beyond the comprehension of those voters who are digging through the fridge for a beer. Try the late-night TV commercial style to really grab the voters' attention.

"Crazy———'s running for president! What a deal! Everything is slashed in half: unemployment, inflation, budget deficits, privileges for the rich, inequalities, bad manners—all out the window! Everybody gets his share of the government! I've got cabinet posts! I've got judgeships! I've got staff appointments and every public works job you could imagine! I've got so many jobs I'm practically giving them away! We're open twenty-four hours in our grand voter deal-a-thon. Come on down and make the best deal you can. My principles are so low, I've got to . . ."

Well, you get the idea.

If this approach is a little too energetic for you, try Walter Mondale's technique of slipping a commercial into the campaign rhetoric. "Where's the beef?" was probably his most effective line all spring. It may not ultimately win votes, but it sure does sell hamburgers.

Network pollster, preparing to declare the winner for the year 2008

The Everybody Solution

West Coast voters have been discouraged in recent elections because the networks projected winners before the polls were closed, further reducing the incentive to vote. By predicting the winner of the Iowa caucus eleven minutes before it began, television may have achieved the ultimate coup—short of cancelling the election and simply picking the new president.

With everybody running for president, the networks could face a major obstacle this fall—they might actually have to wait for the results. With so many candidates, it will be difficult for anyone to get a clear majority. Another advantage of everybody running is that no one will be left at home to watch TV. Ratings will plummet, and the networks will be forced to return to normal coverage and more pleasant tactics.

Not only are you about to find your place in history, but you will also make life easier for all future candidates. You might even bring quality programming back to television.

Convention Protocol

The best place to be during the convention is with your feet propped up in front of the television, a can of beer in hand. While the major party candidates are busy fighting it out, you can get a head start on the November election.

Think about it. Even if you show up with a few delegates to your credit, they generally aren't bound to you and can vote for whomever they choose. What's more, all but one of the candidates who actually show up at the conventions will leave as losers.

You're an important candidate. You have better things to do with your time than hang around with a bunch of turkeys wearing funny hats. Don't be diverted by these midsummer antics, and don't let them bamboozle you into aligning yourself with either the donkeys or the elephants.

CAMPAIGN TIP: *No. 10*

Know Your Phrases

There is a whole series of tricky words and phrases that are commonly confused by harried candidates. See if you can figure out the difference between the following four pairs without peeking at the answers.

1. Bunting/Punting

2. Yes men/Yuppies

3. Sitting ducks/Sitting presidents

4. Super Sunday/Super Tuesday

1. Bunting is what you hang when you win. Punting is what you do when all else fails. *2.* Yes men do what they're told. Yuppies tell you what to do. *3.* Ducks have feathers. Presidents don't. *4.* We forget. Which one is football?

If your heart is set on a convention, consider forming your own party and inviting the kinds of people you enjoy having around. San Francisco and Dallas are already booked, but most other cities would welcome a convention. Decide whether you want a small, intimate convention or a big bash, and reserve space accordingly.

You'll need some floor managers to handle the convention itself. If you can't afford fancy communications equipment, get some old rabbit-ear TV antennas and a bunch of earmuffs. Tape half a rabbit ear to each set of earmuffs and instruct your floor managers to walk around pretending to listen to their instructions, responding from time to time into imaginary microphones in their lapels.

You can add excitement to your convention by pooling your resources with other Everybody for President candidates and staging delegate fights, platform controversies, vice-presidential rumors and the like. Be sure that everyone understands it's just for show—you can all leave as candidates when the convention is over.

Check Your Vices

Perhaps you're one of those people who always considered being vice-president about as exciting as kissing your sister (or brother, for that matter).

True, the Chief takes all the glory and leaves his veep in a kind of occupational black hole, but the office can serve as the lazy man's road to the White House.

A total of thirteen vice-presidents have eventually moved into the Oval Office, eight of them by replacing a deceased president, but the vice-presidency is no longer the training ground for future presidents that it once was. Since the days of Martin Van Buren, there has been a definite trend against electing former vice-

CAMPAIGN TIP: *No. 00*

Avoid False Steps: Choose Your Shoes Carefully

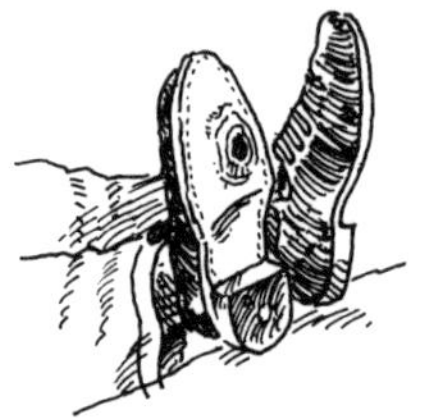

History shows these don't work

Only Reagan can get away with these

Real candidates don't wear loafers

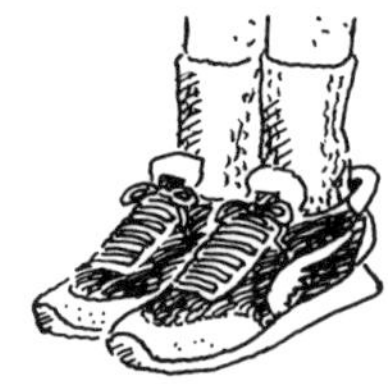

Remember: running for president has nothing to do with running

presidents running on their own merits. In fact, Richard Nixon is the only former vice-president in nearly 150 years to enter the White House through an election.

Deciding whether to run for president or vice-president is a major crossroads in your campaign career planning. Should you keep your record clean and head straight for the top job? Or would you rather bring up the rear and wait for nature to take its course?

There are some definite advantages in forgoing the presidency and running for vice-president from the start. If you enter the vice-presidential race before the major party conventions, you'll have no opposition and can legitimately claim front-runner status. You might even pull off a major political coup and become the first vice-presidential candidate to choose your presidential running mate, instead of the other way around. You can still have all the fun without the responsibility that comes with the top job. True, your salary will be lower, but the benefits are similar.

There is something about the Oval Office that tends to age presidents rapidly—four years in the White House adds about ten years' worth of wrinkles and gray hair. Not so for veeps, who are free to spend most of their time at the health club or lounging around beach resorts as the political equivalent of ladies-in-waiting.

But if you're determined to run for president, at least consider some tips on selecting your veep. For starters, you're best off with a running mate who is such a jerk that nobody would possibly allow anything to happen to you (known in Washington as the Insurance Policy). Nixon had the political wisdom to choose Spiro Agnew for job protection—little did he know that Agnew would be the first to go, giving the country the easy option of Gerald Ford. Had Agnew not gotten caught, we might still have Dick Nixon to kick around.

There are even those who believe a running mate can help you get elected. Despite Reagan's 1976 gaffe of picking Richard Schweiker as his running mate before the delegates got a chance to select their favorite candidate, we at Everybody for President think you'd be much better off with a little company on the campaign trail. If nothing else, vice-presidential candidates are good for carrying luggage, kissing the messy babies, warding off unpleasant people and covering all those out-of-the-way whistle stops that you can't stand.

So, in addition to being someone who makes you look great by comparison, the running mate should have strong arms, an even temperament and a weak disposition. An especially devious ploy, if you find yourself facing stiff competition, is to offer the vice-presidency to your opponent. This could unify your party and clear the path for you at the same time—it certainly puts him on the spot. If you could somehow talk Reagan into becoming your running mate, you might succeed in unifying the entire country.

ON THE ROAD

For the Iowa primaries, before the big money has come in. This compact vehicle offers you high visibility with low maintenance costs. It's great with the young crowd and for chasing down those hard to reach voters. You'll never have to worry about embarrassing parking tickets again. Caution: For Democrats only.

Perfect for convention time, when you need those extra perks to pick up uncommitted delegates. If this doesn't give you that air of importance, then nothing will. It's also good practice for the four years ahead, in case you actually win.

THE HOME STRETCH

Up the Polls

It's a sign of the times that the big names in polling, like Garth, Yankelovich, Caddell and Gallup, loom larger on the political horizon than those of the candidates themselves. Since these heavyweights are usually signed up early by the major parties and the press, here are the essentials for conducting your own polls.

The first question in any survey conducted this election year must necessarily be: "Are you running for president?" The answer will obviously affect the rest of your questions. Assuming your respondent is not also running for president, proceed with the survey, driving straight to the heart of the issues.

You might include questions concerning U.S. policy in Iceland, whether the Rose Garden should be available for private parties and the viability of polyester as the national fabric. Careful phrasing is essential, and respondents require an amusing question or two before they can speak on the larger issues.

The key to successful polling is to ask the kinds of questions that produce the right answers without the respondent having to think too hard. "Do you approve of the current president?" is far too challenging. Instead try: "Do you support the president's self-defeating and utterly useless monetary policy, or do you prefer my farsighted progressive plan for revitalizing the economy and your weekly paycheck?"

To ensure the absolute legitimacy of your results, arrange for your polls to demonstrate a slow but steady increase in support for your campaign right up until the election.

And speaking of support, don't forget that all the undecideds—in your own polls as well as in the better-known surveys—are folks

Special Interests

Candidates are often worried about appealing to special-interest groups. Since Everybody constitutes the largest special-interest group in America, you should avoid any of the other more traditional special interests in your campaign. The following list should help identify the kinds of special interests worth pursuing and those which should be avoided.

Safe	Politically Risky
Golf	Big Labor
Tennis	Oil companies
Travel	NRA
Television	Pro-life
Pro football	Pro-choice
Parties	Nuclear freeze

who are firmly in your corner. Those honest souls whose reply is "I don't know" should be counted as your supporters, and those who don't vote during the primaries may legitimately be looked upon as supporting everybody for president.

Finally, keep in mind that you really don't want to know how you're doing. Gone are the days when polls were done to determine the mood of the people and guide the delicate process of devising campaign strategies. Polls are now just another weapon in the candidate's bag of tricks—a subtle device to help influence the outcome of the election and keep the voters entertained during off-hours.

Party Time

As everybody knows, the best way to find a party is to look for all the parked cars—a hint that seems particularly appropriate considering the stagnant state of the two major parties. As a candidate you'll need to decide whether to align yourself with a specific party or go to as many parties as possible.

The Third Party has a long and noble history in American politics. Abraham Lincoln won as the Third Party candidate. Other notable renegades include: Millard Fillmore, candidate for the Know-Nothing Party (a platform that was hard to argue with); Theodore Roosevelt, leader of the proud Bull Moose group; and other fine statesmen like Robert La Follette and John Anderson.

Starting your own party will virtually assure you of winning the nomination—a definite ego boost and publicity attraction for your campaign. No matter how small your group, you can still claim that prestigious Third Party status. (While there have been dozens of Third Parties, there has never been a Fourth Party—only a Fourth Estate.)

The Debating Club

Front runners and incumbents usually avoid debates like the plague. But this year is different, with the Democratic "If This Is New Hampshire, We All Get Mondale" Traveling Debate Show and an actor-incumbent who never could pass up a chance to be on camera.

The first presidential debate was in 1960, between the clean-cut John Kennedy and unshaven Richard Nixon. Kennedy won the viewers, while Nixon got the support of the listeners. Learn from this example and never debate a candidate who is better-looking than you.

Take a lesson from Gerald Ford, too, and remember to review your geography before appearing on camera. A televised debate is the one place where you must take care not to say anything foolish—you don't have to be brilliant, or even interesting, but you absolutely must not be stupid.

If you manage to debate Reagan, casually leave out in the open a copy of a fake briefing book and see if his staff takes the bait. Unfortunately, the Everybody for President Campaign recently grabbed Reagan's briefing book for 1984 and found it blank. This may mean that Reagan won't debate everybody. In that event, score points by staging your own debate. Prepare all your own statements, and alternate between giving your position and hopping over to the other podium to give what you understand Reagan's position to be. For authenticity's sake, try to keep a straight face when you get to the part about the deficit.

Don't worry about the other candidates. Ignoring them now will be good practice for doing the same when you're the incumbent.

Campaigner's Phrase Book

Because there are nearly as many potentially important issues as there are potential votes, we highly recommend using the Equivocal Myriad Message Matrix method (also known as eenie-meenie-mynie-mo) to determine which critical issues to deal with in extemporaneous speeches.

Although we'd like to claim this convenient decision-making tool as our own, it's been used by politicians in various ways for centuries. We do, however, take credit for the handy grid format.

Cut along the dotted line and keep this chart close at hand. You never know when the press might catch you with your pants down, so to speak. All you do is combine words from each of the three columns to form a total of 729 fresh, provocative issues.

EQUIVOCAL MYRIAD MESSAGE MATRIX

I	II	III
Defeating	Nuclear	Whales
Boring	Illegal	Aliens
Negotiating	Nonsexist	Deficit
Winning	Phased	Labor
Improving	Federal	Communism
Maintaining	High	Taxes
Saving	Diplomatic	Welfare
Paying	Secret	Women
Stonewalling	Skyrocketing	Infrastructures

Vocabulary Builders

Candidate: A job seeker without a resumé (no relation to the root "candid").

Deficit: The gap between what a candidate promises and what he delivers.

Electoral College: Postgraduate institution granting the required degree to the president-elect.

Everybody: You.

Federal budget: A comedy of errors.

Gender gap: A large canyon in Southern California.

Groundswell: An imaginary phenomenon supposedly discovered by candidates.

Heartland: Where Everybody lives, according to the front runner.

Hymie: What you should never call someone if you want his vote.

Incumbent: The one person responsible for all the country's problems.

Inoperative statement: Units of words directly attributable to official spokespeople that have since been determined to be contrary to the best interest of and impacting negative-wise on the immediate advantage of the administration or campaign.

Issues: Irrelevant annoyances.

Mcgovernment: 1. Undigestible policies at inflated prices. 2. What we would have had if McGovern had won.

New ideas: Old ideas.

Pac-Man: A game in which lobbyists gobble up candidates.

Poll vault: Political leapfrog.

Projections: Directives from the media, telling you who to vote for.

Rainbow coalition: Supported by no one in particular.

Real progress: Standing still, but talking fast.

Rose Garden: What voters are frequently promised but never get.

Summit meetings: Impromptu talks at the top of the ski slopes.

Window of vulnerability: What the candidate looks out through.

Speaking to a group of blacks in Montgomery today, Mr. Jackson urged blacks not to vote for Mr. Mondale despite his "good record" on civil rights.

"Some people say they are going to support Mondale because he's going to win," he said. "Well, he ain't. Have as much sense as a rat. A rat jumps off a sinking ship. That's something these rats ought to do."

Campaigning today in the South, the candidates continued their criticism of each other along the lines that made for sharp clashes in Sunda 's nationally ised debate

you shouldn't compare potential supporters to rats

MIAMI, March 12 — "I ... Walte at peace, I'm sort of liberated," F. Mondale said with a faint smile today.

"I got rid of all that front-runner stuff," Mr. Mondale said in an interview. "It's lousy to be a front-runner because people think you don't need them. Now they know I need them."

The former Vice President spent his final day before the voting in nine states in an eight-city campaign visit ties in Florida, Georgia an nly a

Don't tell people you like losing

The Name Game

The name of a product, as any adman can tell you, is often its most important feature, and the selling of the president is no different. Names like Millard Fillmore and Rutherford B. Hayes don't come along every day.

Take a lesson from Carter and avoid being tagged with derogatory nicknames. Jimmy is not such a bad name, but it isn't the way a president should be addressed. Reagan never would have made it if he had allowed "Dutch" to stick. Fritz is okay for a cat.

Another thing to remember about first names is that while Ronald, Franklin, Woodrow and Ulysses all have a unique quality, more people named James have made it to the Oval Office than any others—beating out the Johns by two.

Fortunately, there is a well-established precedent for candidates changing their names—while Hartpence has a Dickensian ring, Hart has the brevity and exuberance of a new spirit.

Just as important as the name itself is name recognition. Since the majority of the electorate is so involved with the daily chores of going to work and watching six and a half hours of television, getting them to recognize and know your name puts you halfway into the White House. Following such logic, the best name for the Everybody candidate would be Smith—there are, after all, over 2.5 million Americans named Smith, constituting a group larger than most unions. All the Smiths in the land would feel a part of your campaign and could even pretend they were related to you. Of course, adding a Jones to your ticket as the vice-presidential candidate would bolster your appeal even further.

First ~~Ladies~~ Persons

Feel free to use this family photo in place of your own

Everybody for President is an equal opportunity campaign. We most emphatically do not discriminate against any presidential candidate on the basis of sex, so let's not jump to conclusions about presidential spouses, okay?

The term "running mate" has been erroneously applied to the vice-presidential candidate for much too long. While you may think you have all the work in running for president, your spouse faces the job of persuading the country that he or she can carry out the important responsibilities of being a first person.

The White House would not be such a desirable place to live without Jackie Kennedy's genteel touch. Lady Bird Johnson helped keep our highways clean—and had a great name to boot. Nancy Reagan is a trendsetter for socialites and Barbie Dolls alike. And Rosalynn Carter ran the country (does that mean Jimmy was the first spouse?).

Remember, the country may judge you more by your family than by your own personality. If your relatives don't fit the bill, then by all means send them on a vacation and circulate this first family photo we've prepared for you.

The Real Party

The most important thing you can do to celebrate your election is to buy a case of champagne (domestic) on Monday, since all the bars are closed on Election Day.

Next, attend to your Balloting Plans. Candidates generally capitalize on what is often their last day of nonstop media coverage by taking a whole troop of reporters into the ballot booth. Unfortunately, this means getting up early, because for some reason voters like to see that their candidate can look good first thing in the morning—it provides that last-minute reassurance that sometimes helps you nab those "undecideds."

Once in the voting booth, please remember that while you may have supported Everybody throughout the campaign, you cannot actually vote for everybody—you must vote for somebody, most reasonably yourself. After that, you can take the rest of the day off and relax before getting all dressed up for your victory celebration. Find out where the opposition's campaign party will be held, so you know where to go in case you didn't buy enough champagne the day before. This will also help you identify which party is yours and which is theirs, saving an unnecessary last-minute embarrassment.

It's the little considerations like these that will distinguish your presidency as organized and thrifty in the eyes of friends and adversaries alike.

Back to College

Our founding fathers had great faith in democracy . . . but not quite enough to trust the people with selecting their president. In a hilarious undermining of the voting process, they gave the real say in the matter to a small, sophomoric organization, appropriately called the Electoral College.

The joke is on both the candidates and the voters. It turns out that after as many as four years of campaigning, the expenditure of untold millions and balloting from February to November, the votes cast don't necessarily mean a thing (something citizens have suspected all along). Over the years the electoral system has given us a total of fifteen presidents who won less than half of the popular vote.

Everybody can run, but only the 535 electors actually elect the president. Now do you see why they were so willing to let you run?

Of course, the electors are supposed to vote for the candidate who carries their home state, but nothing in the Constitution requires them to vote that way. Some states are a little more honest than others about all this and don't even bother to put the names of the presidential candidates on their ballots—they only list the electors.

For the lazy (or perhaps just clever) candidate, the thing to do is wait until the general election is over, find out who the electors are and then start your big campaign push. You'll have all that money you didn't spend earlier, and your strategy should take the competition (and perhaps even the electors) by surprise. The electors cast their votes on the first Monday after the second Wednesday of December (that's December 17 to regular people), so you have plenty of time to win them over. Keep in mind that the Electoral College has no campus—it's strictly a correspondence school.

You'll have one more chance to make a comeback when Congress officially counts the votes on January 6. If nobody carries the Electoral College by a majority, the House of Representatives gets to take a crack. Imagine, the fate of the presidency left in the hands of a bunch of lame duck congressmen (full of spite and envy if they weren't re-elected themselves). What's a candidate to do?

The only lesson from the Electoral College is, it's not over till it's over.

White House Pet Policy

The sweet taste of victory.

We've done it. We ran for president and here we are, sipping Perrier while the moving company packs the parakeet, toaster oven and other essentials for the move to 1600 Pennsylvania Avenue.

Oh yes, you'll have to make plans for the care of the presidential seal. The Secretary of State is the keeper of the Great Seal of the United States, but the Presidential Seal is for the exclusive use of the president.

We can tell you now that the seal is playful and will want to take an occasional splash in the Jacuzzi or a romp in the Oval

Office. The White House swimming pool will be a perfect home, but be careful if important guests go swimming. Seals bite and they have cold, inquisitive noses.

Everybody for President has been a friendly, cooperative campaign from the outset, and we hope this mood will prevail now that Everybody has won. A fresh approach for the new administration would be to turn the White House into a time-share condominium and institute a "president of the day" policy to let everybody have a turn at safeguarding democracy.

This will put the country back in the hands of the people and allow you to concentrate on the main task facing any president—running for re-election.

Campaign Extras

The EVERYBODY FOR PRESIDENT campaign staff is ready to help you in your pursuit of the Oval Office. Write directly to campaign headquarters for all those extras that will really impress your friends.

PLEASE SEND ME:

***Candidate business cards:** Includes our seal, White House address/phone, personalized with your name/address/phone.

☐ 50 for $12.50 ☐ 100 for $17.50

***Deluxe candidate certificate:** Two-color, framable (8½ x 11), personalized with your name.

☐ $3.00 each _____ quantity

Inaugural ball invitations: Adds a presidential touch to your social gatherings, envelopes included with fold-over cards.

☐ 10/$5.00 ☐ 25/$10.00

Campaign trail note pads: Keep your friends up-to-date with presidential notes, fifty 5½ x 8½ sheets in each pad.

☐ $1.50 each ☐ $6.00 for 5 _____ quantity

☐ YES send my *free* copy of the EVERYBODY FOR PRESIDENT campaign newsletter

*PERSONALIZED ITEMS: Please print name, address and/or phone you want on certificates and candidate business cards.

SEND TO:

_______________ postage/handling $ 1.00

_______________ Colo. Residents add 6% sales tax $ _______

_______________ **Total enclosed** $ _______

☐ MasterCard ☐ Visa _______________

Interbank # (M.C. only) _______________ Expiration Date _______________

Authorized Signature _______________

Enclose payment with order

Address all correspondence to: **Gil Campbell/Martha Gorman**
Everybody for President Campaign
P.O. Box 175
Niwot, Colorado 80544